REMEMBER THE PARABLES

Published by CWR, Waverley Abbey House, Waverley Lane, Farnham, Surrey GU9 8EP.
Reprinted 2004.
The right of Jonathan Lee to be identified as the author and illustrator of this work has been asserted by him in accordance with the Copyright, Designs and Patents Act 1988.

Bible verses taken from the Good News Bible © American Bible Society 1966, 1971, 1976, 1992, 1994.

See back of book for list of National Distributors.

Concept development, editing, design and production by CWR.

Illustrations: Jonathan Lee

Printed in England by Linney Print

ISBN: 1-85345-301-3

REMEMBER THE GOOD SAMARITAN

Written and illustrated by Jonathan Lee

Another busy Friday afternoon was coming to an end. The class settled on the reading carpet as Mrs Phips opened the Bible to read a story told by Jesus many years ago. She cleared her throat, 'Uh hum', and began to read . . .

... There was once a very **happy** man, who had a very **happy** donkey and plenty of food ... which made him **very happy.**

One day he and his donkey were walking down the road from Jerusalem to Jericho, happy as can be and whistling with glee. All was peaceful and quiet when all of a SUDDEN...

They ripped his clothes, took all he had
and left him there cut and bruised.

Some time later, a priest walked by on the same road. He saw the man lying there hurt and bruised and all alone.

You would expect the priest to stop and help.
But he didn't, he just walked on by.

A few more moments passed when a teacher of the Law called a Levite came by. Surely he would stop to help the poor man! ...

But he didn't. He also walked on by.

The poor **unhappy** man was left alone once more, **hurting** bruised, and about to give up all hope, when ...

... a Samaritan came by. His heart was filled with pity when he saw the poor man lying there all alone, so he ...

... bandaged his wounds ...

. . . let him ride on his donkey . . .

... and took him to a place where he could get better. The Samaritan gave the

nnkeeper two silver coins to look after the poor man until he was well again.

Thanks to the Samaritan's kindness the unhappy man soon became **happy** again ... and so too did his donkey.

As the story ended, Mrs Phips closed the Bible and said,

'So then children, we also should be like the good Samaritan.'

Just then, a little girl called Hannah put her hand up and said,
'But Mrs Phips, I never see anyone lying on the side of the road,
hurt and bruised, and who's just had their donkey taken away'.

Mrs Phips thought for a while, smiled at Hannah and replied . . .

'Well, Hannah, when you see someone upset, . . .'

'... or feeling sad,'

'... or hurt, ...'

'... remember the good Samaritan'.

REMEMBER THE ~
~ GOOD SAMARITAN

LUKE Ch 10 v 25-37. Fill in the missing words and l e t t e r s to find out who was kind to the poor and hurt man ⟿

⟿ The Priest and Levite both... v31 [　　　]

[　] BY, ON THE [　　　] [　　　].

... But when the good Samaritan saw the poor and hurt man his... 'v33 h _ _ _ _ _ w _ _ _ i _ l _ d _ _ _ t _ f _ _ _ _ _ ....' So he...

v34

_ _ a _ d _ g _
_ i _ _ _
_ w

_ _ _ o o _ _ _ _ m
_ _ o _ _
_ _ n _ _

...and...

u _ _ h _
_ _ s
o _ k

...and...

COLOUR IN PAGES

MEMORY VERSE ~ 'This, then, is what I command you: love one another.' (John Ch 15 v 17)

Titles in this series

The Lost Sheep
ISBN: 1-85345-302-1

Remember the First Christmas
ISBN: 1-85345-317-X

£3.99
each (plus p&p)

The Wise and Foolish Builders
ISBN: 1-85345-303-X

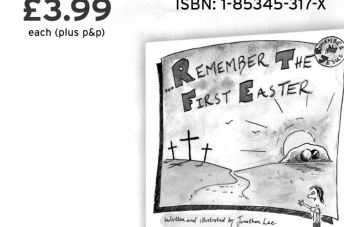

Remember the First Easter
ISBN: 1-85345-330-7

National Distributors

UK: (and countries not listed below)
CWR, Waverley Abbey House, Waverley Lane, Farnham, Surrey GU9 8EP.
Tel: (01252) 784700 Outside UK (44) 1252 784700

AUSTRALIA: CMC Australasia, PO Box 519, Belmont, Victoria 3216.
Tel: (03) 5241 3288

CANADA: Cook Communications Ministries, PO Box 98, 55 Woodslee Avenue, Paris, Ontario.
Tel: 1800 263 2664

GHANA: Challenge Enterprises of Ghana, PO Box 5723, Accra.
Tel: (021) 222437/223249 Fax: (021) 226227

HONG KONG: Cross Communications Ltd, 1/F, 562A Nathan Road, Kowloon.
Tel: 2780 1188 Fax: 2770 6229

INDIA: Crystal Communications, 10-3-18/4/1, East Marredpalli, Secunderabad – 500026, Andhra Pradesh.
Tel/Fax: (040) 27737145

KENYA: Keswick Books and Gifts Ltd, PO Box 10242, Nairobi.
Tel: (02) 331692/226047 Fax: (02) 728557

MALAYSIA: Salvation Book Centre (M) Sdn Bhd, 23 Jalan SS 2/64,
47300 Petaling Jaya, Selangor.
Tel: (03) 78766411/78766797 Fax: (03) 78757066/78756360

NEW ZEALAND: CMC Australasia, PO Box 36015, Lower Hutt.
Tel: 0800 449 408 Fax: 0800 449 049

NIGERIA: FBFM, Helen Baugh House, 96 St Finbarr's College Road, Akoka, Lagos.
Tel: (01) 7747429/4700218/825775/827264

PHILIPPINES: OMF Literature Inc, 776 Boni Avenue, Mandaluyong City.
Tel: (02) 531 2183 Fax: (02) 531 1960

SINGAPORE: Armour Publishing Pte Ltd, Block 203A Henderson Road,
11–06 Henderson Industrial Park, Singapore 159546.
Tel: 6 276 9976 Fax: 6 276 7564

SOUTH AFRICA: Struik Christian Books, 80 MacKenzie Street,
PO Box 1144, Cape Town 8000.
Tel: (021) 462 4360 Fax: (021) 461 3612

SRI LANKA: Christombu Books, 27 Hospital Street, Colombo 1.
Tel: (01) 433142/328909

TANZANIA: CLC Christian Book Centre, PO Box 1384, Mkwepu Street, Dar es Salaam.
Tel/Fax (022) 2119439

USA: Cook Communications Ministries, PO Box 98, 55 Woodslee Avenue, Paris, Ontario, Canada.
Tel: 1800 263 2664

ZIMBABWE: Word of Life Books, Shop 4, Memorial Building,
35 S Machel Avenue, Harare.
Tel: (04) 781305 Fax: (04) 774739

For email addresses, visit the CWR website: www.cwr.org.uk

CWR is a registered charity – number 294387